PRICE GUIDE

PRESSED TABLEWARE

Most glass produced in Sandwich factories was clear, so expect the price of colored objects to be high. Reproductions issued by museum gift shops have contaminated the antiques market. Learn where the "repros" were signed. Inspect for damage that may indicate the removal of a museum "logo".

Photo No.	Clear	Clambroth (Alabaster)	Opaque White	Canary	Amber	Blue	Amethyst	Green	Unusual Color
1001 a	75								
b	60					150 pale			
1002 a	125					350			
b	125					350			
c	150					425			
1003	400						1200		
1004	100								
1005	60								
1006 a	60								
b	180								
1007	150								
1008	200								
1009	100								
1010	375								
1011 a	100								
b	—								
1012	900								
1013	3700								
1014 a	110								
b	40								
1015	40					200			
1016	35					350			
1017 a	35								
b	30								
1018 a	450								
b	35								
1019	500								
1020	20								
1021	65						450 pale		
1022	1000								
1023	300								
1024	325								

Photo No.	Clear	Clambroth (Alabaster)	Opaque White	Canary	Amber	Blue	Amethyst	Green	Unusual Color
1025	35								
1026 a	300								
b	35								
1027	400								
1028	1100								
1029	3800								
1030 a	1000								
b	—								
1031	2000			13,000		16,000	13,000		
1032	1400								
1033 a	40			200		200	275	275	
b	40			200		200	275	275	
1034	40			200		200	275	275	
1035	175								
1036	1000								
1037 a	45								
b	38								
1038	35				300	225	250	300	
1039 a	500					1200			
b	40	350 fiery opalescent					400		
1040	200	1800		2500		3000	3000	3500	5000+
1041	200	3500 fiery opalescent							
1042	500	700				1750 opaque	2000		
1043	500					5000			6000
1044	300								
1045	90								
1046	200	500 fiery opalescent							
1047	5500								
1048	1200								
1049	2100					5500			
1050	500	1600	600			5500	5500	6500	
1051	5200			15,000		12,000		18,000	
1052	6500			20,000					
1053	1000			2000		3600			
1054	650								
1055	90					400			
1056	185	1600 fiery opalescent	500	2000		2500			
1057	35	110	110	350	375	375	375	500	800
1058 a	35	110	110	350	375	375	375	500	800
b	600			2000	2500	2500	2500	3500	
1059 a	35			225		375	375	450	
b	600			2000		2500	2500	3500	
1060	38								
1061 a	500								
b	350								

Photo No.	Clear	Clambroth (Alabaster)	Opaque White	Canary	Amber	Blue	Amethyst	Green	Unusual Color
1062	7500								
1063	7500								
1064	600					6000			
1065	650					2100			
1066	525								
1067	50			275 pale					
1068 a	475								
b	80								
1069	90								
1070	125								
	1250 silver nitrate								
1071	110			1800		2000			
1072	60								
1073	—								
1074	150								
1075 a	600								
b	600								
1076	150								
1077	1800								
1078	2400								
1079	400					12,000			
1080	600								
1081	5000								
1082	600								
1083	400					2250			
1084	200	750	900	1000		1400	1800	2800	
1085	35			400		500	600		
1086 a	100			875		875			
b	—								
1087	200			1800		3000			
1088	150						500 pale		
1089	150								
1090	285								
1091	110								
1092	80								
1093	450								
1094	80								
1095	110								
1096	875								
1097	50					300			
1098	35								
1099	175								
1100	1000								
1101	185								
	1800 silver nitrate								
1102	300							750	
1103	450								
1104	125								

Photo No.	Clear	Clambroth (Alabaster)	Opaque White	Canary	Amber	Blue	Amethyst	Green	Unusual Color
1105	125								
1106 a	200								
b	80								
1107	80	500 fiery opalescent							
1108	80								
1109	60	125 fiery opalescent				250	350		
1110 a	80	480 fiery opalescent				500	650		
b	35	100 fiery opalescent						200 pale	
1111 a	1000								
b	80	480 fiery opalescent				500	650		
1112	90					500			
1113 a	120			1050					
b	90			875					
1114	140			1200					
1115 a	375								
b	100								
1116	65 110 gilded								
1117	165			1000		1500			
1118	165								
1119 a	100			600		500			
b	75			300					
1120	150			700					
1121	500								
1122	250								
1123	250								
1124	185								
1125	525								
1126	850	12,000 fiery opalescent		25,000			30,000	40,000	44,000
1127	22			95		135			
1128	25						140		
1129 a	15					95			
b	18						190		
1130	65				400		400		1200
1131	65								
1132 a	85								
b	30			125		200			
1133	3500			8000			12,000	15,000	
1134	85			875		1100		1500 peacock	
1135	135			900		1500			

Photo No.	Clear	Clambroth (Alabaster)	Opaque White	Canary	Amber	Blue	Amethyst	Green	Unusual Color
1136 a	50			900	1200	900	950	1200	
b	45			1200	1200	900	950	1200	
1137	75			875					
1138	65								
1139	85								
1140	50						825		
1141	190			2000		3200	4200		
1142 a	40			450		500			
b	—								
1143	235	1800 fiery opalescent		2500		3500 peacock		4500	
1144	250			2000		3500			
1145	15			100		150	190		
1146	225			2400		2500	4700		
1147	225			2500		2500	5500		
1148	225			1600		2200	4500		
1149	225			1600		2200	4500		
1150	95			750					
1151	180			2800					
1152 a	300			1800					
b	—								
1153	180			3200		7500	8000	12,500	
1154	35 ea.								
1155	225			1200					
1156	100	400 fiery opalescent							
1157	235	650 fiery opalescent							
1158	60	275 fiery opalescent					300		
1159	65 ea.			875 ea.					
1160	300 pr.								
1161	235								
1162	250								
1163 a	50			875		1000	1000		
b	50			875		1000	1000		
1164	50 ea.			875 ea.		1000 ea.	1000 ea.		
1165 a	60								
b	50								
1166	40		250	250		400			
1167	190			1800		2000			
1168	200			2200					
1169	190			3200					
1170	200			1200					
1171	300								
1172	800								
1173	65			1200					
1174	1800								
1175	800			5000		6500	7500		
1176	1500			10,000		15,000	18,000	25,000	

Photo No.	Clear	Clambroth (Alabaster)	Opaque White	Canary	Amber	Blue	Amethyst	Green	Unusual Color
1177	90								
1178	110 without stopper			1600 without stopper		2000 without stopper			
1179	85 ea.	250 ea.	250 ea.	900 ea.		1200 ea.			
1180	100			900			1200		
1181 a	100			1000		1200	1400		
b	100			1000		1200			
1182 a	140								
b	90								
1183	35								
1184	160		800						
1185	100	1200 fiery opalescent							
1186 a	75								
b	75								
1187 a	135	900 fiery opalescent				1500			
b	275								
1188	90			875		1200			
1189	190						1200 light		
1190 a	—								
b	30								
1191 a	235								
b	285								
1192	75								
1193	85								
1194	60	550 fiery opalescent		500					
1195	160		200			525			
1196 a	135								
b	135								
1197	135					400			
1198 a	125								
b	—								
1199	—								
1200 a	135 175 engraved								
b	20 ea. 26 ea. engraved								
1201	15 ea. 18 ea. engraved								
1202 a	40 without label								
b	—								
1203 a	110								

Photo No.	Clear	Clambroth (Alabaster)	Opaque White	Canary	Amber	Blue	Amethyst	Green	Unusual Color
b	115								
c	105								
d	150								
1204 a	210								
b	125 without cover	125 without cover	300 without cover	575 without cover		600 without cover		750 without cover	
c	85								
1205	195								
1206	80 ea.								
1207	45 ea. without cover	235 ea. without cover fiery opalescent							
1208 a	45								
b	—								
1209	—								
1210	85 engraved								
1211 a	45			125		100	185	300	
b	60			135		135	250	400	
c	100						325		
1212 a	150								
b	175								
1213	85								
1214	250		450						
1215	85		950			2500			
1216 a	85								
b	150		575						
1217	—								
1218	225								
1219	45								
1220	90								
1221	375								
1222 a	120								
b	375		650						
1223 a	135								
b	185								
1224 a	85								
b	125								
1225 a	135								
b	185								
1226	55								
1227	125								
1228	110								
1229	60	215 250 gilded				900 1100 gilded		1100 1300 gilded	
1230	200								
1231 a	160								
b	185								
1232 a	35								
b	30								

Photo No.	Clear	Clambroth (Alabaster)	Opaque White	Canary	Amber	Blue	Amethyst	Green	Unusual Color
1233	500 pr. 575 pr. engraved								
1234 a	135								
b	160								
1235	165								
1236	85 235 decorated	300						750	
1237 a	600								
b	550								
1238	525								
1239	150								
1240 a	135								
b	—								
1241	20								
1242	85								
1243 a	160								
b	115								
1244	325 the set								
1245	50								
1246	50								
1247	55								
1248	35								
1249	60								
1250 a	40 60 gilded								
b	60 80 gilded								
1251	145 165 gilded								
1252 a			100						
b			65						

FREE-BLOWN AND BLOWN MOLDED TABLEWARE

Most glass produced in Sandwich factories was clear, so expect the price of colored objects to be high. Blown objects have been heavily reproduced. It is difficult to find originals on the open market. Objects accompanied by family documentation are worth up to three times more.

Photo No.	Clear	Clambroth (Alabaster)	Opaque White	Canary	Amber	Blue	Amethyst	Green	Unusual Color
1253	450								
1254	130					550	650		
1255	325 with stopper								
1256 a	110			1000		1200	1400		
b	80			900		1000	1200		

Photo No.	Clear	Clambroth (Alabaster)	Opaque White	Canary	Amber	Blue	Amethyst	Green	Unusual Color
1257	400								
1258	40								250
1259	38 ea.			75 ea.	75 ea.	75 ea.			
1260	38 ea,			75 ea.	75 ea.	75 ea.			
1261		100 opal decorated							
1262	250								
1263	180								
1264	155								
1265	525					1500			
1266	750								
1267	700								
1268	6500								
1269	6500								
1270	—								
1271	5200								
1272	6000								
1273	125								
1274 a	45 with stopper								
b	—								
c	45 with cap								
1275	125					400	525		
1276	45					525	600		
1277	55								
1278 a	200								
b	—								
1279	110 ea.					500 ea.	525 ea.		
1280 a	125					500	525		
b	125					500	525		
1281 a	235								
b	185								
c	185								
1282 a	70								
b	70								
1283	—								
1284	750 the set								
1285	—								
1286	300 with cap								
1287	—								
1288	110					450			
1289	235								
1290	235							300 pale	
1291	450								
1292	150					375			
1293 a	150					375			
b	185					750			
1294	275								

Photo No.	Clear	Clambroth (Alabaster)	Opaque White	Canary	Amber	Blue	Amethyst	Green	Unusual Color
1295	750								
1296	300								
1297	300								
1298	400								
1299	600								
1300	1700					2500			
1301	600								
1302	900								
1303	300								
1304	235								
1305 a	400								
b	30								
1306 a	225								
b	225								
1307	275								
1308	300								
1309	8500					13,000			
1310	200								
1311	500								
1312	400								
1313	300								
1314	600								
1315	190								
1316 a	220								
b	220								
1317	400								
1318	210								
1319 a	275								
b	75								
1320 a	190								
b	175								
1321	700								
1322	225								
1323 a	185					600			
b	750					3200	4500		
1324	600								
1325	575					2200	3000		
1326	575					3200			
1327	235								
1328	115								
1329	250								
1330	250								
1331	235 ea.								
1332	1200 the set								
1333	700					4500	4000		
1334 a	200					5000			
b	200					5000	5000		
1335	1000					6000			
1336	450								
1337	140 without stopper								
1338 a	300								

Photo No.	Clear	Clambroth (Alabaster)	Opaque White	Canary	Amber	Blue	Amethyst	Green	Unusual Color
b	850								
1339 a	2500								
b	850								

PRESSED CUP PLATES

A cup plate with a pontil mark is a base that was broken away from a lamp or candlestick. It should not be highly valued. The invention of the cap ring allowed the number and shape of rim scallops to vary on the same pattern cup plate. This variation does not indicate a rare example and does not affect value of a given cup plate pattern. Value is not affected by slight changes in pattern due to handwork by the mold maker. Prices given for unrecorded colors may be for variants.

Photo No.	Clear	Clambroth (Alabaster)	Fiery Opalescent	Opaque White	Amber	Blue	Amethyst	Green	Unusual Color
1340 a	50								
b	—								
c	85					500			
d	85								
1341	185								250 pale pink
1342 a	135					900			
b	175								
1343 a	135								
b	50								
c	50					1000			
d	50					900			
1344 a	75								
b	95								
c	85								
1345	75				450				
1346	75								
1347	60		175					1200 pale	
1348	75		275						
1349	100						700		2100 black
1350	—								
1351	2000								
1352	60		250 blue						
1353	80								
1354	90					1500 silver-blue			
1355	100			500		1500 silver-blue			
1356	100					1500 silver-blue			
1357	100					1500 silver-blue			
1358	—								
1359	60								
1360	60								
1361	75								
1362	75								

Photo No.	Clear	Clambroth (Alabaster)	Fiery Opalescent	Opaque White	Amber	Blue	Amethyst	Green	Unusual Color
1363	75								
1364	50							450	
1365	70		210			300 opalescent			
1366	100					450		650	
1367	75								
1368	75								
1369	95 ea.	150 ea.	210 ea.						
1370	110								
1371	90					650 550 pale	750 550 pale		
1372	95					875 peacock			
1373	75								
1374	55	100		150					
1375	475								
1376	—								
1377	50			250		600			
1378	65					750		875	
1379	165		325			600		875	
1380	80			200		400	400	550	
1381	35			275				600 pale	
1382	65	165					225 pale		
1383	25								
1384	25								
1385	45		135		300		375		
1386	85					325 pale			
1387	85								
1388	75								400 canary
1389	65					550			
1390	75								
1391	75								
1392	90	150						375	
1393	95								
1394	80								500 canary
1395	75					750	700 light	750	
1396	60					425		750	
1397	65					400	500		
1398	45					400		750	875 canary
1399 a	50						750		
b	50	190				250		750	
1400	55								1200 opaque green
1401	45						450	750	
1402	70	150					450		

Photo No.	Clear	Clambroth (Alabaster)	Fiery Opalescent	Opaque White	Amber	Blue	Amethyst	Green	Unusual Color
1403	45								
1404	50					450			
1405	50				325	375 375 peacock	250 light	400 400 peacock	
1406	65	150		150	700 red-amber		300		750 dark amber
1407	65					400 400 pale		650 650 pale	375 yellow- green
1408	25	250					225 pale		
1409	30						225 pale		
1410	30					400			
1411	30		210			325			
1412	350								
1413	35					450		450 pale	
1414	35		325		400	400			
1415	35				500	425			750 citron
1416	100				775	800			
1417	100				775	800			
1418	85				600	700 600 peacock		350 pale	
1419	75	150				325			
1420 a	800 silver nitrate center								
b	2000 silver nitrate border								
1421	2000 silver nitrate								
1422	100	200				400		1400	
1423	90					950			
1424	40					500			750 canary
1425	50							2500	
1426	90					1000		3500	
1427	135							1000	
1428	80							325	

OPEN AND SHAKER SALTS

Plain, heavy open salts made during the first decade of production do not command the prices of intricately molded Lacy pieces. An intense color is worth more than a pale color. Expect to pay more for shakers with patented devices that break up the salt. A slight variation in a mold due to handwork by a mold maker does not affect value. Prices given for unrecorded colors may be for variants.

Photo No.	Clear	Clambroth (Alabaster)	Fiery Opalescent	Canary	Amber	Blue	Amethyst	Green	Unusual Color
1429	35								
1430	350								
1431	250					600			
1432	300					600			
1433	450 without cover					1500 without cover			
1434 a	650 without cover					1500 without cover			
b	400					1600			
1435	150					950			
1436	90							450	
1437 a	25								
b	—								
1438 a	25								
b	—								
1439	55				325	325		550 yellow- green	700
1440	65					325		550	700
1441	65					325			700
1442 a	60					700			
b	60					700			
1443	90	250	250			500 600 silver-blue			
1444	175	450	450			700			
1445	160					750 875 silver-blue			
1446	40							350 light	
1447	110	200	280		500	500		650	1000
1448	90 without cover	200 without cover				300 without cover	350 without cover		550 without cover
1449	800	900				2500	2750		
1450	135					600			700
1451 a	800		900			2500		2750	
b	—								
1452	175								
1453	250		500		875			1800	
1454	325							600 pale	
1455	110	225	475						
1456	80				150	175	200		
1457	80				300	175			

Photo No.	Clear	Clambroth (Alabaster)	Fiery Opalescent	Canary	Amber	Blue	Amethyst	Green	Unusual Color
1458	100								
1459	100				400	350		500	650
1460 a	185					900 silver-blue			
b	175					700			
1461	135					1100 silver-blue			300 opaque white
1462	75					400 pale			
1463	450	800				1200			
1464 a	450					1400 silver-blue 1400 opalescent			
b	450	800	1700			1200			
1465	135	400	400			500	600		900
1466	80	135	300			475		600	
1467	150					575			
1468	150					575			
1469 a	225					1200			
b	225		900			1200			
1470 a	225								
b	—								
1471	80				350 750 red-amber			700	2000 black
1472	30				200	250	250		
1473	30				200	250	250		
1474 a	50								
b	—								
1475 a	25								
b	—								
1476	40 ea.					185 ea.		250 ea. peacock	
1477	60								
1478 a	75					500			
b	250								
1479 a	75					500			
b	110								
1480	80			125		325			
1481	200								
1482	125 185 frosted								
1483	100								
1484	150								
1485	90 ea.		150 ea.	235 ea.		425 ea.			
1486	8 ea. 1000 twelve in box	12 ea.			12 ea.	12 ea.			
1487 a	45					125	150		
b	—								

Photo No.	Clear	Clambroth (Alabaster)	Fiery Opalescent	Canary	Amber	Blue	Amethyst	Green	Unusual Color
1488 a	45	60 opaque				125	150		
b	—								
1489	80					90	100		
1490 a	—								
b	8	16 opaque				25			
1491	125 ea.								
1492	125								
1493	110 silvered engraved								
1494	110 silvered engraved								
1495 a	65	75 opal		150	150	200	275	250	600 ruby
b	65	75 opal		150	150	200 250 peacock	275	250	600 ruby
c	175 two-bottle frame								
1496	240 the set	275 opal the set		350 the set	400 the set	525 the set	650 the set	650 the set	1200 ruby the set
1497	85	95		175	175	275 peacock	300	275	625 ruby
1498		125 ea. opal decorated							
1499 a	75				175	175	325	325	
b	75				200	200	375	375	
1500 a		110 opal decorated							
b		110 opal decorated							
1501		115 ea. opal decorated							
1502		450 opal decorated the set							
1503		250 pr. opal decorated							
1504						175 spangle			

LIGHTING DEVICES

Most early whale oil lamps were clear, so expect the price of colored lamps to be extremely high. Many early lighting devices will be priced in clear glass only. Expect to pay more for objects accompanied by documentation.

Photo No.	Clear	Clambroth (Alabaster)	Opaque White	Canary	Amber	Blue	Amethyst	Green	Unusual Color
2001	525								
2002	900								
2003	1100								
2004	1200								
2005	1200								
2006	1400								
2007	6500								
2008	3800								
2009	600								
2010	600					3500			
2011	900					4200			
2012 a	45					150			
b	1000					3800			
2013	2250					3500			
2014	2250								
2015	1400					5500 blue and clear			
2016	1200								
2017 a	1400								
d	1000								
2018	1000								
2019	300								
2020	1800 pr.					20,000 pr.			
2021 a	250								
b	250								
c	300								
2022	525								
2023	750 pr.								
2024	750 pr.								
2025	750								
2026	850								
2027	—								
2028	800								
2029	800								
2030	2400 pr.								
2031	900								
2032	1200					8500			
2033	1350								
2034 a	185								
b	1200								
2035	1200								
2036	1500					10,000		20,000	
2037 a	140								
b	1100								
2038	1600 pr.					20,000 pr.			
2039 a	650								
b	600								
c	—								
2040	2250 pr.								

Photo No.	Clear	Clambroth (Alabaster)	Opaque White	Canary	Amber	Blue	Amethyst	Green	Unusual Color
2041	650								
2042	—								
2043	900								
2044 a	7500								
b	3800								
2045 a	900								
b	800								
2046 a	750								
b	600		900			4600 opaque			
2047	600								
2048	450				2250	2800 blue and clear		3200 green and clear	
2049	400								
2050	150								
2051	400								
2052	900 pr.								
2053	900 pr.								
2054	300								
2055	300								
2056	250 pr.								
2057	300								
2058	300								
2059	1200 pr.								
2060	1400 pr.								
2061	1200 pr.								
2062	2400 pr.								
2063	300								
2064	1200 pr.								
2065	1200 pr.								
2066	1200 pr.								
2067	700								
2068	1400 pr.								
2069	1400 pr.								
2070	2500 pr.								
2071	—								
2072	300			1000					
2073	—								
2074	—								
2075	—								
2076	500		875						
2077	700		1500			4500 silver-blue			
2078	350								
2079	950 pr.		1800 pr.						
2080 a	110								
b	—								
2081	300								
2082	—								
2083	575								
2084	450								
2085 a	300		1000			2000	1800		
b	250		800				2200		

Photo No.	Clear	Clambroth (Alabaster)	Opaque White	Canary	Amber	Blue	Amethyst	Green	Unusual Color
2086 a							12,000 in box		
b	300		1000			2000	1800		
2087	110								
2088	300					900			
2089	40								
2090 a	100								
b	110								
2091	110								
2092	400 pr.			1400 pr.	3000 pr.	3000 pr.	3200 pr.	4200 pr.	5000 pr.
2093 a	235			750	1200	1200	1200	1750	
b	200			450		900			
2094	235			900		1200	1400	2000	
2095	12,000								
2096	—								
2097 a	235			900		1400	1600	2500	
b	250			900		1400	1600	2500	
2098	235			900		1400	1600	2500	
2099	—								
2100	235			900		1400	1400	2000	
2101	575 pr.			1800 pr.	3000 pr.	3200 pr.	3200 pr.	4200 pr.	
2102 a	235			700	1200	1400	1400	2000	
b							1400		
2103	235			700	1200	1400	1400	2000	
2104 a	250			1000		2500	2500	4200	
b				225					
2105	180			800		1400	1400	2250	
2106	140					850	1000	1400	
2107	200	250	500			900	800	1200	
2108	200		600						
2109 a	350								
b	350			875	1850	1500	1500	2500	
2110	575 pr.			2800 pr.	5000 pr.	3600 pr.	3600 pr.	6500 pr.	
2111 a,b	600 pr.			2000 pr.		3600 pr.	3600 pr.	7500 pr.	
c	225			850		1400	1400	2800	
2112	—								
2113 a	175			650		1000	1000	1500	
b	175			650		1000	1000	1500	
2114	260 pr.			1400 pr.		2200 pr.	2400 pr.	3200 pr.	
2115	575 pr.								8500+ pr. peacock green
2116	200	1400 fiery opalescent		950		1400	1400	2000	
2117	390	1700 fiery opalescent		1200		1600	1600	2000	
2118	250	1200	1000	1200		1500	1500	2500	
2119 a	250	1200	1000	1200		1500	1500	2500	
b	60					1400			
2120	250	1200	1000	1200		1500	1500	3000	
2121	650 pr.	3000 pr.	3000 pr.	4000 pr.		6500 pr.	6500 pr.	9500 pr.	

Photo No.	Clear	Clambroth (Alabaster)	Opaque White	Canary	Amber	Blue	Amethyst	Green	Unusual Color
2122	100 burner								
2123						10,000 blue and white			
2124	—								
2125	10 ea.								
2126 a	180								
b	180					1400			
2127 a	160								
b	75								
2128	1400					6500			
2129	300								
2130	4500								
2131	—								
2132	10,000 pr.								
2133	600								
2134 a	350			800			1200		
b	350			900			1200		
c	350								
2135 a	750 pickwick								
b	350 pickwick								
2136	360 pickwick								
2137	290			900					
2138 a	250								
b	235								
2139 a	250								
b	325								
2140	500								
2141	75								
2142	400								
2143	400								
2144	12,000 pr.		20,000 pr.	22,000 pr.		28,000 pr.	28,000 pr.		38,000 pr.
2145		4500	5000	6000		7500	7500	10,000	
2146	—								
2147	950 pr.	1200 pr.		2250 pr.		6500 pr. 7000 pr. blue and white	6500 pr.	8500 pr. green and white	
2148 a	500								
b	350	400		700					
2149	—								
2150 a	500								
b	400	575				1400 blue and white		2200 green and white	
2151 a	400	575				1400 blue and white		2200 green and white	
b	700								

Photo No.	Clear	Clambroth (Alabaster)	Opaque White	Canary	Amber	Blue	Amethyst	Green	Unusual Color
2152 a	75 burner								
b	100 burner								
c	150 burner								
2153	125 burner								
2154 a	150 burner								
b	150 burner								
2155	100 burner								
2156	85 hook								
2157	150	250				600		750	
2158	—								
2159	600 the set	1200 the set				2000 the set		2400 the set	
2160	650 pr. with burners					3200 pr. with burners blue and white			
2161	110	1500 fiery opalescent				1500 blue and clear			
2162 a	450								
b	60								
2163 a	235								
b	—								
2164	150								
2165	175								
2166	—								
2167 a	235								
b	235								
2168	750 pr.								
2169	750 pr.	1600 pr. gilded							
2170 a	450								
b	425								
2171	575								
2172	250								
2173	275								
2174	300								
2175	500 with teapot								
2176	200 teapot with burner								
2177	400								

LAMP SHADES AND GLOBES

The shape of a shade or globe is not as important as the design that may be cut, engraved, painted or transferred onto it. The price is determined by the intricacy of the design. Prices do not reflect family documentation. Expect to pay three times these prices for objects accompanied by family documentation.

Photo No.	Price	
2178	235	
2179	1100	the set of lamp glasses
	5000	with lamps
2180	450	pr.
2181	2500	the shade
2182	—	
2183	—	
2184	—	
2185	85	
2186	300	
2187	300	
2188	—	
2189	300	
2190	—	
2191	300	
2192	—	
2193	100	
2194	100	
2195	300	
2196	300	
2197	300	
2198	450	
2199	450	
2200	—	
2201	—	
2202	450	
2203	—	
2204	450	
2205	—	
2206	150	
2207	150	
2208	300	
2209	90	
2210	150	
2211	195	
2212	195	
2213	225	
2214	400	with fixture
2215	600	
2216	75	
2217	125	
2218	—	
2219	80	
2220	200	
2221	190	
2222	35	
2223	35	
2224	25	
2225	75	
2226	60	the globe
2227	85	
2228	175	
2229	195	
2230	175	
2231	175	
2232	160	
2233	140	
2234	130	
2235	140	
2236	150	
2237	160	
2238	150	

LIGHTING DEVICES

Multiple combinations are possible when lamps are assembled by joining fonts to bases with metal connectors. Therefore, the price will reflect only the lamp that is pictured. Expect to pay more for objects accompanied by documentation.

Photo No.	Price	
2239 a	875	
b	700	
2240 a	875	
b	225	
2241	325	
2242	1000	
2243	185	
2244	—	
2245	10,000	
2246	750	
2247	450	
2248 a	300	
b	—	
2249	110	
2250	175	
2251	3200	
2252	200	
2253	1000	
2254	300	
2255	175	
2256	110	
2257	210	
2258 a	235	
b	250	
2259	200	complete
2260 a	9500	
b	10,000	
2261	14,000	
2262	—	
2263	10,000	
2264	500	peg lamp
2265	—	
2266	35,000	with white opal globe
	38,000	with blue opal globe
	40,000	with lavender opal globe
2267	—	
2268	235	
2269	50	burner
2270 a	250	
b	275	
2271 a	250	
b	250	
2272	500	
2273 a	50	
b	20	
c	50	burner
2274 a	450	
b	450	
2275	—	
2276	250	
2277	250	
2278	625	
2279	375	
2280	50	
2281	275	
2282	—	
2283	1250	pr.
2284	4800	

Photo No.		
2285		700
2286	a	575
	b	575
2287	a	185
	b	300
	c	175
2288		400
2289		70 burner and tripod
2290		60 wicks in box
2291		35 scissors
2292	a	650
	b	600
2293		350
2294		300
2295		750
2296		700

Photo No.		
2297		1500
2298		1800
2299		—
2300		1400
2301		12,000
2302		1600
2303	a	1000
	b	1200
2304		500
2305		900
2306		600
2307		500
2308		600
2309		—
2310		750
2311		200

Photo No.		
2312		1600
2313	a	150 pr.
	b	60 ea.
2314		725
2315		250
2316		—
2317		250
2318		—
2319		175
2320		350 pr.
2321	a	525
	b	185
2322		600
2323		250
2324		600
2325		—

OVERLAY (PLATED) LIGHTING DEVICES

The workmanship on Sandwich Overlay lamps can be crude. The layers of glass can vary in thickness and the cut designs can vary in size on the same piece. These manufacturing inconsistencies do not deter from value. Expect to pay more for objects accompanied by documentation.

Photo No.		
2326	a	450
	b	450
2327		700
2328	a	110
	b	200
	c	200
	d	200
2329		900
2330		2100
2331		—
2332		2500
2333		—
2334		40
2335		175
2336	a	175
	b	125
	c	100
	d	60
2337		100
2338		60
2339		900
2340		1400
2341	a	1400
	b	1400
2342	a	1400
	b	1200
	c	1200
2343		2750
2344		25,000

Photo No.		
2345		18,000
2346		26,000
2347		6000
2348		5800
2349		900
2350		2750
2351		2000
2352		2800
2353		8000
2354		2400
2355		4800
2356		22,000
2357		20,000
2358		3500
2359		1400
2360	a	950
	b	1200
2361		450
2362		2700
2363		3200
2364		2500
2365		28,000
2366		1200
2367		1400
2368		1200
2369		1800
2370	a	2200
	b	4500
2371		18,000

Photo No.		
2372		12,000
2373		1400
2374		4200
2375		4800
2376		6000
2377	a	1400 lamp
	b	1500 lamp
	a	300 pickwick
	b	300 pickwick
2378		9500
2379		3800
2380		1800
2381		3500
2382		8500 pr.
2383		3800
2384		3000
2385		9000 pr.
2386		1500
2387		2750 pr.
2388		2100
2389		3000
2390		2250
2391		2100
2392		2500
2393		2000
2394		12,000
2395		2750
2396		1800
2397		1750

SUSPENSION LAMPS AND LANTERNS

Lanterns are priced as if the name appearing on the globe cannot be identified. Expect to pay more for documented objects.

Photo No.	
2398	1200
2399	—
2400	900
2401	—
2402	4000
2403	—
2404	110
2405	180
2406	250
2407	250
2408	180
2409	80
2410	250
2411	110
2412	150
2413	225
2414	2000
2415	—
2416	6000
2417	—
2418	—
2419	—
2420	750
2421	800
2422	800
2423	—
2424	1200
2425	—
2426	2200
2427	200
2428	225

SMOKE SHADES AND BELLS

Most smoke shades and bells have an applied glass ring by which they are hung. If the hanging ring is damaged in any way, the value of the object is lost. Small bells have metal hanging rings. Do not purchase small bells that are missing their metal rings. It is impossible to find replacement metal fittings.

Photo No.	
2429	90
2430	115 with chain
2431	100
2432	95
2433	120
2434	100 with hanger
2435	115
2436	110
2437	60 with chain
2438	35
2439	40
2440	125
2441	160
2442	165
2443	110
2444	150
2445	200
2446	200
2447	90
2448	275
2449	200
2450	160
2451	200
2452	200
2453	200
2454	200
2455	180
2456	35
2457	75
2458	110
2459	110
2460	110
2461	100
2462	125
2463	125
2464	—
2465	125
2466	—

ELECTRIC LIGHTING

Photo No.		
2467	a	200
	b	—
2468	a	75
	b	75

VASES AND FLOWER CONTAINERS

A single vase is worth less than 50 percent of a matching pair. When you are pricing vases, make sure you have a matching pair and not two single vases. Unlike candlesticks and lamps, vases that were pressed were made in single colors only. Expect to pay more for documented objects.

Photo No.		Clear	Clambroth (Alabaster)	Opaque White	Canary	Amber	Blue	Amethyst	Green	Unusual Color
3001	a	90			575		800	800	800	
	b	15 ea.			18 ea.		20 ea.	20 ea.	20 ea.	30 ea. ruby

Photo No.	Clear	Clambroth (Alabaster)	Opaque White	Canary	Amber	Blue	Amethyst	Green	Unusual Color
3002				1000 pr.		1000 pr.	1200 pr.	1400 pr.	
3003		180 fiery opalescent		180	180	180	200		400 lime green
3004		180 fiery opalescent			180	180	200		400 lime green
3005	20			80		80	80		
3006	45								
3007	300								
3008	2000 pr.								
3009	135								
3010	150								
3011	135								
3012	140								
3013	150								
3014	100 ea.	100 ea.	100 ea.	250 ea.		275 ea.	300 ea.	400 ea.	600 ea.
3015	250 pr.	300 pr.	300 pr.	400 pr.		550 pr.	650 pr.	800 pr.	1000 pr.
3016	15		40			80	100	150	
3017	800 pr.			2000 pr.		2500 pr.	2800 pr.	3800 pr.	6000 pr.
3018	325 ea.			900 ea.		1800 ea.	1800 ea.	2000 ea.	4500 ea.
3019	750 pr.			5000 pr.		7000 pr.	7000 pr.	9000 pr.	
3020	450 pr.						6500 pr.		
3021	85 ea.	2500 ea. fiery opalescent		875 ea.	1000 ea.	1200 ea.	1000 ea.	1200 ea.	1500+ ea.
3022	85 ea.	2500 ea. fiery opalescent		875 ea.	1000 ea.	1200 ea.	1000 ea.	1200 ea.	1500+ ea.
3023	85 ea.	2500 ea. fiery opalescent		875 ea.	1000 ea.	1200 ea.	1000 ea.	1200 ea.	1500+ ea.
3024	200								
3025	600			1000	2800	2250	2250	3200	
3026				3200 pr.	3200 pr.	2500 pr.	2500 pr.	3500 pr.	
3027		750		3100	3200	3500	3000	3200	
3028				3100	3200	3500	3000		
3029	100 ea.			1000 ea.		1500 ea.		3100 ea.	
3030	500 pr.			2800 pr.		5500 pr.	4800 pr.	7500 pr.	
3031	300			800					
3032				1000		1550	1550		
3033	450 pr.	1200 pr.		2200 pr.		3500 pr.	3500 pr.	7500 pr.	
3034	500 pr.			3800 pr.		4200 pr.	4500 pr.	7000 pr.	
3035	400			2200			3000		
3036				2200			3000		
3037 a	250			1000			2500	3500	
b							2500		
3038		600		900					
3039	450 pr.			2250 pr.		4800 pr.	4800 pr.	6000 pr.	
3040	200			800		1400		1400	
3041	110	1400 fiery opalescent	1200	1500	2000	2000	2000	2250	

Photo No.		Clear	Clambroth (Alabaster)	Opaque White	Canary	Amber	Blue	Amethyst	Green	Unusual Color
3042	a	235			900		1200	1400	2500	
	b	235			900		1200	1400	2500	
3043	a			1000 pr.			1400 pr.		1600 pr.	
	b			525			525		625	
3044	a			1000 pr.			1400 pr.		1600 pr.	
	b		300 ea. with fitting	300 ea. with fitting			300 ea. with fitting	300 ea. with fitting	300 ea. with fitting	
3045			185							
3046	a						1750 ea. blue and white		1750 ea. green and white	
	b						1750 ea. blue and white		1750 ea. green and white	
3047							1750 ea. blue and white		1750 ea. green and white	
3048	a		180				400	480	600	
	b						400			

Photo No.		
3049		4500 pink to white to clear Overlay, gilded
3050		200 clear 500 opal, decorated
3051		225 ea.
3052		500
3053		500
3054		1500 the set
3055		200 ea.
3056		110
3057		110
3058		110
3059		150
3060		225 pr.
3061		100
3062		110
3063		160
3064		110
3065		100
3066		—
3067		—
3068		—
3069		50

Photo No.		
3070		40
3071		70
3072		90
3073		450
3074		300
3075		450
3076		450 undecorated 500 gilded 650 decorated, colored flowers
3077		525 decorated, blue ground 525 decorated, brown ground 650 decorated, lilac ground
3078	a	90
	b	75
	c	60
3079		125
3080		250
3081		—
3082		1000
3083		2200

Photo No.		
3084		3500
3085		—
3086		—
3087		3500
3088	a	1500 stand
	b	3500 ea.
	c	3500 ea.
3089	a	50
	b	28
	c	20
3090		190
3091		190
3092		50
3093		60
3094		50
3095		60
3096		125 ea.
3097		25 ea. holder
3098		90
3099		22 clear 110 fiery opalescent
3100		125 clear 175 fiery opalescent

COLOGNES

Cologne bottles used on dressing tables have glass stoppers. More than half the value of a cologne is in its stopper. Expect to pay as much as three times more for documented objects. Prices for commercial colognes are included with prices for bottles, beginning with photo No. 5182.

Photo No.	Clear	Clambroth (Alabaster)	Opaque White	Canary	Amber	Blue	Amethyst	Green	Unusual Color
3101	150 ea.	350 ea.		525 ea.		1500 ea.		2500 ea.	
3102	150	350		525		1500		2500	
3103	225			500		1200		2200	
3104				1200		1600			
3105	90			300					
3106	115		250	500					
3107	110				1000	1000		1500	
3108	190 pr.	450 pr. fiery opalescent			800 pr.			1450 pr. light	
3109	90	230			300			500	
3110				800 ea.	900 ea.	1000 ea.		1200 ea.	
3111	180					875			
3112	150			600	800	875	900		
3113	135			750		900		1200	
3114								1200	
3115						1100			
3116			450						
3117				300		400			
3118 a	90					400	400	750	
b	80			250				675	
3119						750		950	
3120				450		750		750	
3121 a						1400 with underplate			
b		70				110			
c		300 with fitting	300 with fitting			300 with fitting	300 with fitting	300 with fitting	
3122						225 blue and white		225 green and white	250 yellow and white
3123						400 blue and white		575 green and white	
3124								600	
3125		225				525		625	
3126								1100	

Photo No.	
3127	450
3128	—
3129	150
3130	250 with stopper
3131	190
3132	195

Photo No.	
3133	195
3134	195
3135	900 blue to clear Overlay
3136	825 blue to clear Overlay
	825 ruby to clear Overlay
3137	1000 blue to clear Overlay

Photo No.	
3138	1000 blue to clear Overlay
3139	1000 blue to clear Overlay
	1100 ruby to clear Overlay
3140	1600 blue to clear Overlay
	1500 ruby to clear Overlay
	1600 green to clear Overlay
3141	1200 blue to clear Overlay
3142	1600 blue to clear Overlay
	2000 ruby to clear Overlay
3143	2000 ruby to clear Overlay
3144	—
3145	2000 ruby to clear Overlay
3146	1800 amethyst to clear Overlay
3147	1600 ruby to clear Overlay
3148	2300 ruby to clear Overlay
3149	2250 ruby to clear Overlay, with correct stopper
3150	2000 ruby to clear Overlay
3151 a	100 ruby to clear Overlay
b	100 blue to clear Overlay
3152	2200 pr. blue to clear Overlay
	1900 pr. ruby to clear Overlay
	2200 pr. green to clear Overlay
3153	250 clear
3154	800 blue to clear Overlay
	900 canary to clear Overlay

Photo No.	
	800 ruby to clear Overlay
	800 green to clear Overlay
3155	800 ruby to clear Overlay
3156	1000 ruby to clear Overlay
3157	2300 ruby to clear Overlay
3158	700 pink to white to clear Overlay
3159	1000 pink to white to clear Overlay
3160	200 ruby stained
3161	200 ruby stained
3162	200 ruby stained
3163	200 ruby stained
3164	200 ruby stained, with correct stopper
3165	575 pr. ruby stained
3166	400 ruby stained
3167	325 clear Overshot
	600 blue Overshot
	600 pink Overshot
3168	600 blue Overshot
	600 pink Overshot
3169	125
3170	110
3171	550 green threads on green
3172	550 ruby threads on clear, engraved
3173	185 ruby threads on clear, with correct stopper

STOPPERS

A container that has its correct stopper often will double in value. The purchase of stoppers known to be Sandwich is an investment that will pay handsomely from time to time.

Photo No.	Clear	Clambroth (Alabaster)	Opaque White	Canary	Amber	Blue	Ruby	Amethyst	Green
3174	5 ea.								
3175	5 ea.								
3176 a	5 ea.				15 ea.				
b					15 ea.				
c					15 ea.				
3177	20 ea.				50 ea.	40 ea.		40 ea.	
3178	20 ea.					40 ea.		60 ea.	
3179	20 ea.								
3180 a	—								
b	50 ea.								
3181	15 ea.					125 ea.			
3182	15 ea.								
3183 a	15 ea.								
b	20 ea.								
c	15 ea.								
d	15 ea.								
3184	30 ea.								

Photo No.	Clear	Clambroth (Alabaster)	Opaque White	Canary	Amber	Blue	Ruby	Amethyst	Green
3185	5 ea.								
3186	5 ea.								
3187	5 ea.								
3188	5 ea.								
3189	800								
3190 a	5 ea.								10 ea. pale
b	5 ea.								10 ea. pale
c	5 ea.								10 ea. pale
3191					1200				
3192					10 ea.				
3193				10 ea.	10 ea.		30 ea.		15 ea.
3194	5								
3195 a	—								
b	100 ea.								
c	100 ea.								
d	100 ea.								
e	100 ea.								
3196	80 ea.								
3197	80 ea.								
3198	90 ea.								
3199	90 ea.								
3200	90 ea.								
3201	10 ea.						80 ea.		
3202	10 ea.								
3203 a	—								
b	5 ea.								
c	5 ea.			15 ea.	20 ea.	25 ea.		25 ea.	
3204 a	10 ea.			50 ea.	80 ea.	100 ea.	200 ea.	100 ea.	200 ea. dark
b	10 ea.			50 ea.	80 ea.	100 ea.	200 ea.	100 ea.	200 ea.
3205	10 ea.								
3206 a	15 ea.			25 ea.	25 ea.				
b	15 ea.			25 ea.					
c	15 ea.		15 ea.		25 ea.				
3207	15 ea.			25 ea.	25 ea.	60 ea.			
3208 a	15 ea.			25 ea.	25 ea.	60 ea.			
b	15 ea.			25 ea.					
3209 a	10 ea.								
b	10 ea.			35 ea.		35 ea.			60 ea.
c	15 ea.			35 ea.		35 ea.		50 ea.	
d	15 ea.			35 ea.	35 ea.	35 ea.	100 ea.	50 ea.	100 ea.
3210 a	30 ea.			75 ea.	100 ea.				
b	30 ea.				100 ea.				125 ea.
c	30 ea.				100 ea.				125 ea.
3211		100 ea.				125 ea.			125 ea. custard
3212 a									150 ea.
b						100 ea.			
c						100 ea.			
3213	5 ea.			25 ea.	25 ea.	30 ea.		35 ea.	

Photo No.	Clear	Clambroth (Alabaster)	Opaque White	Canary	Amber	Blue	Ruby	Amethyst	Green
3214	6 ea.				25 ea.			35 ea.	
3215	5 ea.			20 ea.	30 ea.	30 ea.		35 ea.	
3216	5 ea.			25 ea.		30 ea.		35 ea.	35 ea.
3217	5 ea.			25 ea.	25 ea.	25 ea.		35 ea.	

Photo No.		
3218	a	18
	b	20
	c	20
	d	20
3819	a	75
	b	50
	c	60 ruby threads on clear
	d	20
3220	a	50
	b	30

Photo No.		
	c	50 ea.
3221	a	60 ruby threads on clear
	b	100 ruby threads on clear
	c	75 ruby threads on clear
	d	60 ruby threads on clear
3222	a	200
	b	200
3223	a	200
	b	200
3224		—

BALLS

Photo No.		
3225		1400
3226		1100
3227		1100 pink loops
		600 white loops
3228		2250
3229		1200
3230		300
3231		300
3232		300
3233	a	300
	b	150

Photo No.		
3234		1600 with extension
3235		1800 with extension
3236		450
3237		50 ea.
3238		50 ea.
3239	a	50 ea.
	b	800
3240		50 ea.
3241		—
3242		225 ea.

COVERED CONTAINERS

Little value remains to a container that has lost its cover. Keeping covers in pristine condition guarantees maximum return on the dollar spent for containers.

Photo No.	Clear	Clambroth (Alabaster)	Fiery Opalescent	Opaque White	Canary	Amber	Blue	Amethyst	Green
3243	5800				15,000		18,000		
3244	700				1400		1500		
3245	6500				15,000		15,000		
3246	—								
3247	6500				15,000		15,000		
3248	—								
3249	600				1200		1200		
3250	4250				15,000				
3251				12,000			28,000		30,000
3252	—								
3253	1800	2500		3000	5500		6500		7500
3254	—								

Photo No.	Clear	Clambroth (Alabaster)	Fiery Opalescent	Opaque White	Canary	Amber	Blue	Amethyst	Green
3255				750			900		
3256				350					
3257				400					
3258				500 with cover					
3259					1500		2250	2250	
3260		1800		2000	1800		3800	3800	5500
3261 a		1200		1400			3500	1500	
b		1000		1100			2800	750	
c		600		800	2000		2250	400	
3262		600		800	2000		2250	400	
3263 a		1200					3800	1500	
b	—								
3264		100							
3265	220						1200		1500
3266	300	550					1400		1800
3267 a	—								
b	220						1400		1800
3268 a	220	550					1200		1800
b	90	190					500		600
3269	190	400			1100		1400		1800
3270	190	550		600	1200		1400		1600
3271 a	90	90		150	275		450		600
b	60								
3272	235 with cover						1100 with cover		
3273	235				800		900		
3274	275			550	900				
3275	150								
3276	110 ea.			300 ea.	500 ea.		600 ea.		
3277 a	—								
b				80					
3278	750						1400	1600	2500
3279				550			900		
3280 a	150			300	650		700		800
b	150			300	650		700		800
3281	—								
3282 a	65	90		90			150		225
b	65	110		110			160		225
3283	100			150			300	300	
3284	150	180	200		250	300	350	400	
3285					900		1000		1000
3286	—								
3287							1000		
3288	—								
3289	150	375	475		650		875		
3290	750 ruby to clear Overlay								
3291	110		185				400	600	

Photo No.	Clear	Clambroth (Alabaster)	Fiery Opalescent	Opaque White	Canary	Amber	Blue	Amethyst	Green
3292 a	85		135						
b	85		135				300		
3293 a	85		135				300		
b	85		135						
3294 a	85		135						
b	85		135				300		
3295			55						
3296				20 ea.					
3297				250					
3298				85					
3299	110 ea.	135 ea.		135 ea.	200 ea.		375 ea.		500 ea.
3300	—								

TOYS

Glass toys made during the Nineteenth Century were intended for children's play. Expect to find more roughage than is found on adult tableware. The value does not drop as rapidly when toys are chipped or damaged.

Photo No.	Clear	Clambroth (Alabaster)	Fiery Opalescent	Opaque White	Canary	Amber	Blue	Amethyst	Green
3301	750 with burner						1800 with burner		
3302	800 with burner						1800 with burner		
3303 a	45						150		
b	900 with burner						2000 with burner		
3304	2500 with burner								
3305	1400 with burner						2750 with burner		
3306	2400 complete								
3307	70								
3308 a	150						450		
b	350						750		
3309	450								
3310	3500								
3311	1800						2500		
3312	1800						2250		
3313	1800						2250		
3314	1800						2250		
3315	750								
3316	450 the set						1400 the set	1600 the set	
3317	450 the set		900 the set		900 the set	2000 the set	2000 the set	2000 the set	3200 the set
3318	200 ea.		475 ea.		600 ea.	1200 ea.	750 ea.	750 ea.	1200 ea.

Photo No.	Clear	Clambroth (Alabaster)	Fiery Opalescent	Opaque White	Canary	Amber	Blue	Amethyst	Green
3319	450 the set				900 the set		2000 the set	2000 the set	
3320	45 ea.	115 ea.	150 ea.		195 ea.		250 ea.	250 ea.	250 ea.
3321 a	45 ea.	115 ea.	150 ea.	195 ea.	195 ea.		250 ea.	250 ea.	250 ea.
b	75 ea.								475 ea.
c	45 ea.	115 ea.	150 ea.	195 ea.	195 ea.		250 ea.	250 ea.	250 ea.
3322	475								
3323	35 ea.				100 ea.	200 ea.	150 ea.	150 ea.	200 ea.
3324	35 ea.				100 ea.	200 ea.	150 ea.	150 ea.	200 ea.
3325 a	18				90	160	150	150	200
b	28				150	200	275	275	275
3326	28				100	200	150	150	225
3327	28				100	200	150	150	225
3328 a	35						200	200	
b	75 pressed handle 100 applied handle						200 pressed handle 275 applied handle	200 pressed handle 275 applied handle	300 pressed handle 350 applied handle
3329	38 ea.	200 ea.					285 ea.	285 ea.	350 ea.
3330	200								
3331	250								
3332	225								
3333	95								
3334	38 ea.	110 ea.					150 ea.	175 ea.	250 ea.
3335	38						150		250
3336 a	100		350				550	600	700
b	75		275				450	475	500
3337	225 the set				800 the set		1200 the set	1200 the set	1500 the set
3338	100	250	285		600		950	950	
3339	130	250	400		750		1200	1400	2000
3340	75	200	200		300	600	400	600	
3341	75 ea.	200 ea.	200 ea.		300 ea.	600 ea.	400 ea.	600 ea.	
3342	150						950		
3343	325								
3344	75 ea.	175 ea.	175 ea.		500 ea.		950 ea.	950 ea.	1200 ea.
3345	450 ea.				900 ea.		1200 ea.	1500 ea.	2000 ea.
3346 a	150						300		
b	175								
3347	425 with underplate		1000 with underplate		1400 with underplate		2000 with underplate	2500 with underplate	2800 with underplate
3348 a	95		175		500		600	750	
b	95		175		500		600	750	
3349	90 ea.		125 ea.		275 ea.		650 ea.	675 ea.	
3350 a	95		160		350		395	425	
b	75		125		300		350	385	
3351	200				700		1200	1200	
3352	200								
3353 a	50								
b	55								
3354	450								

Photo No.	Clear	Clambroth (Alabaster)	Fiery Opalescent	Opaque White	Canary	Amber	Blue	Amethyst	Green
3355	300 the set								
3356	350 the set, in box								
3357	235 the set								
3358 a	25 with cap								
b	25 with cover								
c	25 with stopper								
3359	40 ea.				100 ea.				
3360	500 pr.		2500 pr.		3000 pr.		4000 pr.	5500 pr.	5500 pr.
3361	300 ea.		750 ea.		1800 ea.		1750 ea.	1750 ea.	2200 ea.

Photo No.	
3362	200 ea. multi-colored
3363	150 opaque white
3364	750 clear
3365	9000 clear
3366 a	300 canary
b	1200 Vasa Murrhina
c	750 ruby
3367	500 Vasa Murrhina
3368	500 ruby to clear Overlay
3369	—
3370	195 ea. clear
3371	250 ruby to clear Overlay

CREATIONS OF NICHOLAS LUTZ

Photo No.	
3372	—
3373	—
3374	—
3375	—
3376	—
3377	—
3378	—
3379	—
3380	—
3381	—
3382	—
3383	800
3384	1200
3385	1400
3386	750
3387	800
3388	1400
3389	—
3390	900
3391	900
3392	1000
3393	3000 pr.
3394	1000
3395	500
3396	900
3397	900
3398	800
3399	4500
3400	250
3401	110
3402	350 ea.
3403	10,000
3404	250 ea.
3405	800
3406	50
3407	—
3408	90–150 ea.
3409	90–150 ea.
3410	90–150 ea.
3411	125–175 ea.
3412	—
3413	500
3414	125 ea. with documentation
3415	25
3416	—
3417	—

CANDLESTICKS

A single candlestick is worth less than 50 percent of a matching pair. In most instances, a two-color candlestick is more valuable than the same form made in one color.

Photo No.	Clear	Clambroth (Alabaster)	Opaque White	Canary	Amber	Blue	Amethyst	Green	Unusual Color
4001	12,000								
4002	—								
4003	600 pr.								
4004	650 pr.								
4005	350								
4006	325					18,000			
4007	1000 pr.								
4008	1400					13,000			
4009	4200								
4010	700 pr. including inserts			3200 pr. including inserts			6200 pr. including inserts		
4011	750 pr.								
4012	750 pr.			3200 pr.				16,000+ pr.	
4013	2500 pr.						20,000+ pr.		
4014	1600 pr.								
4015	450 pr.			1800 pr.		1800 pr.			
4016	100			650					1200+
4017	400 pr.			1100 pr.		1500 pr.			
4018	125			500		750			
4019	400 pr.			1100 pr.		1500 pr.			
4020	95			225		600			
4021	300 pr.			700 pr.			1600 pr.		
4022 a	115			235			700		
b	110			225			600		
4023	375 pr.	500 pr.		950 pr.	1200 pr.	2000 pr. blue and white		2400 pr. green and white	3000+ pr.
4024	300 pr.			700 pr.	1400 pr.	1800 pr.	1600 pr.	3200 pr.	
4025	325 pr. candlesticks 250 pr. peg lamps								
4026	325 pr.			700 pr.		1800 pr.	1600 pr.	3200 pr.	5000+ pr.
4027	325 pr.	700 pr.		1100 pr.	1200 pr.	2750 pr.	2750 pr.	3200 pr.	
4028	325 pr.	700 pr.		1100 pr.	1200 pr.	2750 pr.	2750 pr.	3200 pr.	
4029	110	225		275			700		
4030	110	225		275			700		
4031	110			235					
4032	225 pr.	475 pr.	550 pr.	425 pr.	1200 pr.	2250 pr.	2250 pr.	3200 pr.	3600+ pr.
4033 a	195	650		1100			2500		
b	195			1600			3000		
4034	—								
4035	—								
4036	120			190		700	750	1500	2000+
4037	120			190		700	750	1500	2000+
4038	190	300	300	350		1000 blue and white		1500 green and white	

Photo No.		Clear	Clambroth (Alabaster)	Opaque White	Canary	Amber	Blue	Amethyst	Green	Unusual Color
4039	a	700					3500		3500	
	b	190	300	300	350		1500		1600	3500+
4040		190	300	300	350		1500		1600	3500+
4041	a	500					2500 1600 blue and white		2600 green and white	
	b	450					1200 blue and white		1800 green and white	
	c	500					1400 blue and white		2250 green and white	
4042		125	275		450	700	950	950	1250	1000+
4043		—								
4044	a	400		900	1200	1800	1800	2100	2500	3000+
	b	90								
4045		1200		1700	2000	3200	3200	3500	3750	4500+
4046		300 pr.	350 pr.	375 pr.	850 pr.	1100 pr.	1400 pr.	1400 pr.	2000 pr.	2500+ pr.
4047		300 pr.	350 pr.	375 pr.	850 pr.	1100 pr.	1400 pr.	1400 pr.	2000 pr.	2500+ pr.
4048		300 pr.	400 pr.	400 pr.						1500+ pr.
4049		3800		7500	8000		9000	9000		14,000
4050			4500	5000	6000		7500	7500	10,000	
4051		110	135	200	325	425	1000	1000	1200	1600+
4052		250 pr.	500 pr.	550 pr.	700 pr.		2250 pr.	2250 pr.	3200 pr.	4000+ pr.
4053		100	135	200	325	425	1000	1000	1200	1600
4054		550 pr.	950 pr.	1000 pr.	1200 pr.		5500 pr.	6500 pr.	8000 pr.	9000+ pr.
4055		550 pr.	950 pr.	1000 pr.	1200 pr.		5500 pr.	6500 pr.	8000 pr.	9000+ pr.
4056	a	200	350	400	500		2250	2500	3000	
	b						1800 blue and white		2000 green and white	
4057		—								
4058	a						1800 blue and white		2000 green and white	
	b	200	350	400	500		2250	2500	3000	
4059							2500 blue and white, gilded			
4060		900					4000 blue and white		5000 green and white	
4061		450				2000				
4062		—								
4063		750								
Fig. 5		1200 with turban socket								
4064		100								

INSULATORS

Photo No.	
4065	75 ea. with collar
4066	110 ea. with cap and collar
4067	60 ea. with collar
4068	60 ea. with clamp
4069	—
4070	—
Fig. 8	200

Photo No.	
4071	2100
4072	—
4073	500 clear 1000 pink 1000 green
4074	—
4075	—

OVERSHOT (FROSTED WARE)

Examine carefully for damage when considering a purchase. Any damage to the rough surface severely affects value.

Photo No.	Clear	Pink	Canary	Amber	Blue	Green	Ruby	"Snakeskin"	Unusual Color
4076 a	400	1600							
b	380	1200							
4077 b	240 ea.	800 ea.			900 ea.				
4078	300	750			1200				
4079 a	225	800							
b	200	550							
4080	110 ea.	350 ea.							
4081	110	350		1000					
4082	110 ea.	350 ea.							
4083	110 ea.	350 ea.							
4084 a	150	250			825				
b	200	350			900				
4085	200	275							
4086 a			500 with blue handle						
b	150 with amber handle								
4087	135 ea.			200 ea.	300 ea.				400 ea.
4088 a	90	350		200	300				
b	110	250			250				
c	80	235			225			900	
4089	90	350			300	650			
4090 a	200	500			600				
b	50 ea.	150 ea.			175 ea.				
4091 a	225				700				
b	200	500			600				
4092 a	135						875		
b	150 with amber handle				400 with amber handle				
4093		500 pr.							
4094 a	300								
b	275								
4095	235	525							

Photo No.		Clear	Pink	Canary	Amber	Blue	Green	Ruby	"Snakeskin"	Unusual Color
4096	a	65	135							
	b	50	110							
	c	75								
	d	40 with stopper								
4097	a	50	90							
	b	90	110							
4098		300	400			575				
4099		75	190							
4100		190		600						
4101		190								
4102		235								
4103		90			525	525				
4104		110	200		400	450				
4105		110	200		400	450				
4106		125	275			395				
4107		875								

VASA MURRHINA

Photo No.	
4108	1100
4109	—
4110	200
4111	—
4112	750
4113	200
4114	400
4115	—

Photo No.	
4116	400
4117	—
4118	1200
4119	—
4120	500
4121	—
4122	175

Photo No.	
4123	—
4124	125
4125	—
4126	—
4127	—
4128	—
4129	—

4130–4155 Cut or engraved by N. Packwood in Sandwich, but not *manufactured* by Packwood.

4156–4176 Cut or engraved by J. B. Vodon and Son in Sandwich, but not *manufactured* by Vodon.

LATE BLOWN WARE

There are five levels of value.

- The price based on the type of object and its etched or engraved design.
- The addition of a monogram that cannot be traced back to the original owner of the object reduces the base price.
- The addition of a monogram with documentation that traces the object back to the original owner adds to the base price.
- A presentation piece that is completely documented, with a monogram, complete name, date, or special design, is valued significantly higher than any of the above. Expect to pay two or three times these prices for objects accompanied by family documentation.
- Colored objects are very scarce and should be priced accordingly.

Photo No.		
4177	100	
4178	50	
4179	40	ea.
4180 a	40	
b	40	
c	40	
4181	45	
4182	40	
4183	40	
4184	90	
4185 b	525	jar
4186	45	
4187	—	
4188	525	
4189	12,000	
4190	—	
4191	40	
4192	40	
4193	40	
4194	135	
4195	50	
4196	65	
4197	500	
4198	—	
4199	45	
4200 a	45	
b	45	
c	45	
d	55	
e	65	
4201	5	
4202	5	
4203	85	
4204	50	ea.

Photo No.		
4205	75	
4206	185	
4207	425	
4208	450	
4209	35	
4210	95	
4211	30	ea. clear
	115	ea. amber
4212 a	35	
b	30	
c	30	
4213 a	115	
b	110	
4214	18	
4215	140	
4216	75	
4217 a	150	
b	30	ea.
4218	125	
4219	60	
4220	250	
4221	50	ea.
4222	450	
4223 a	90	
b	90	
4224	30	
4225 a	25	
b	30	
c	35	
4226 a	20	
b	20	
4227	75	
4228	115	
4229	15	

Photo No.		
4230	15	
4231	35	
4232	90	
4233 a	125	
b	45	
4234	125	
4235	25	ea.
4236	60	
4237	100	the set
4238	95	
4239	400	
4240	110	
4241	50	
4242	65	
4243	750	the set
4244	110	
4245	110	
4246	650	
4247 a	525	
b	525	
4248	190	
4249 a	120	
b	500	with drainer
c	150	
4250	—	
4251	750	ea.
4252	50	ea.
4253	50	ea.
4254	50	
Fig. 19	25	clear claret
	175	blue claret
Fig. 21	30	clear claret
	235	green claret

4255–4260 Decorated by Edward J. Swann in Sandwich, but not *manufactured* by Swann.

THREADED GLASS

Objects with colored threads on clear bodies have less value than objects with colored threads on colored bodies. The condition of the threads is critical to the value of the object. Etching and engraving adds to value.

Photo No.			
4261	250		blue threads on blue
4262 a	575		ruby threads on clear, engraved
b	125		ruby threads on clear, engraved
4263 a	100		amber threads on amber
b	400		amber threads on amber
4264 a	125	ea.	amber threads on amber, engraved
b	575		amber threads on amber, engraved
4265 a	100		amber threads on amber, engraved
b	575		amber threads on amber, engraved

Photo No.			
4266	125		blue threads on clear
4267	125	ea.	ruby threads on clear, needle etched
4268	100	ea.	clear threads on clear, engraved
4269 a	135	ea.	amber threads on amber, engraved
b	135	ea.	ruby threads on clear, engraved
4270	135	ea.	canary threads on canary, needle etched

Photo No.			
4271		45 ea.	clear, no threads, engraved
4272		100 ea.	ruby threads on clear, engraved
4273		100 ea.	ruby threads on clear, engraved
4274	a	100 ea.	blue threads on clear
	b	120 ea.	canary threads on canary
4275		75	ruby threads on clear, needle etched
4276		75	ruby threads on clear, needle etched
4277		1500	ruby threads on clear, engraved
4278		200	ruby threads on clear, engraved
4279		90	ruby threads on clear
4280		450	ruby threads on clear
4281		375	ruby threads on clear, ruby prunts
4282		250	ruby threads on clear, white inside casing
4283		325	ruby threads on clear
4284		500	ruby threads on clear
4285	a	150 ea.	green threads on green
	b	100 ea.	ruby threads on clear
4286		110	ruby threads on clear, etched
4287		95	ruby threads on clear, etched
4288		135	ruby threads on clear, engraved

Photo No.			
4289	a	90	white threads on pink
	b	95	white threads on pink
	c	150	white threads on pink
4290	a	90	white threads on pink
	b	95	white threads on pink
	c	150	white threads on pink
4291	a	150	white threads on pink
	b	250	white threads on orange
4292		135	ruby threads on clear
4293		175	ruby threads on clear
4294		—	
4295	a	50	blue threads on clear
	b	225	blue threads on clear
4296		250	green threads on green
4297		200	ruby threads on clear
4298		350	ruby threads on clear
4299		90 set	canary threads on canary
4300		35	ruby threads on ruby
4301		85 set	blue-green threads on blue-green
4302		85 set	ruby threads on clear
4303	a	135 set	green threads on canary
	b	45	ruby threads on pale blue
4304		125	ruby threads on clear

4305–4320 Decorated by Mary Gregory. Priced under *Open and Shaker Salts* and *Lighting Devices*.

EPERGNES

Because it is difficult to find completely assembled epergnes, they command high prices. Individual units and incomplete assemblies do not command high prices. Complete epergnes can be assembled by collecting individual units. The result is financially rewarding.

Photo No.		
4321	1500	
4322	1600	
4323	100	base
	200	Frosted Madonna standard with fittings
	60	trumpet with fitting
	60	center plate
4324	250	Frosted Madonna standard attached to base, with fittings
	60	trumpet with fitting
	60	center plate
4325	500	Frosted Madonna standard attached to base, with fittings and center plate
	75	trumpet with fitting
4326	500	Frosted Madonna standard attached to center plate, with fittings
	75	trumpet with fitting

Photo No.			
4327	a	250	with fittings
	b	500	with fitting
4328		—	
4329		—	
4330		—	
4331		500	Frosted Madonna standard with fitting and turban collar
4332		100	
Fig. 28		2500	fish globe with hooks on standard
		2200	fish globe without hooks on standard
Fig. 29		200	clear
		300+	color
Fig. 30		35,000	with white opal globe
		38,000	with blue opal globe
		40,000	with lavender opal globe
Fig. 31		22,500	
4333		2000	

Photo No.		
4334 a	600	with fittings
b	100	with fitting
4335	1800	
4336	1600	
4337	110 ea.	
4338	110	three-hole
	110	six-hole
4339	1600	
4340	350	three-unit assembly with fittings
4341	875	
4342	125	
4343	600	
4344	150	with fitting
4345	100	
4346 a	75	with fitting
b	85	with fitting
c	100	with fitting
4347	800	
4348	250	with fitting
4349	1400	
4350	625	with fitting
4351	100	with fitting
4352	875	
4353	50	with fitting
4354 a	100	with fitting
b	38	with fitting
c	75	with fitting
Fig. 32	3500	
4355	75	with rod and fitting
4356	450	ruby threads on clear
4357	80	with fitting

SANDWICH CO-OPERATIVE GLASS COMPANY

Photo No.	
4358	1000
4359	1250
4360	600
4361	500
4362	350
4363	—
4364	150
4365	80
4366	50
4367	140
4368	45
4369	40
4370	200
4371	3500
4372	550 pr.
4373	125 ea.
4374	500
4375	650
4376	600
4377	600
4378	650
4379	140
4380	375
4381	150

TREVAISE

Photo No.	
4382	2500
4383	—
4384	2500
4385	2500
4386	2250
4387	2000
4388	2200
4389	—
4390	2150
4391	—

CUT, ENGRAVED AND ETCHED GLASS

There are five levels of value.

- The base price, which is given here, is the price based on the type of object and its cut, etched or engraved design.
- The addition of a monogram that cannot be traced back to the original owner of the article reduces the base price.
- The addition of a monogram with documentation that traces the object back to the original owner adds to the base price.
- A presentation piece that is completely documented, with a monogram, complete name, date, or special design, is valued significantly higher than any of the above. Expect to pay two or three times these prices for objects accompanied by family documentation.
- Colored pieces are very scarce and should be priced accordingly.

Photo No.		
5001	450	
5002	350	
5003	300	
5004	475	
5005	1100	
5006	1000	
5007	600	ruby to clear
	700	blue to clear
5008 a	600	
b	1300	
5009	16,000	
5010	3000	
5011	750	
5012	1200	
5013	625	
5014	1000	
5015	2000	
5016	1000	
5017	575	
5018	750	
5019	475	
5020	225	
5021 a	210	
b	200	
5022	75	
5023	135	
5024	175	
5025	300	
5026	1600	
5027	975	
5028	600	
5029	900	
5030	110	
5031	365	
5032	250	
5033	—	
5034	250	
5035	200	
5036	250	
5037	500	

Photo No.		
5038	1200	pr.
5039	900	
5040	3200	
5041	625	pr.
5042	—	
5043	65	
5044 a	525	
b	80	
c	140	
	850	the set
5045	160	
5046	110	
5047	75	
5048 a	200	
b	175	
5049 a	200	
b	80	
5050	35	
5051	225	
5052	600	
5053	150	
5054	110	
5055	475	
5056	150	
5057	225	
5058	110	
5059	300	ea.
5060	150	the set
5061	475	
5062	275	
5063	275	
5064	275	
5065	750	
5066	275	
5067	575	
5068	1100	
5069	80	
5070	100	
5071	100	
5072	650	

Photo No.		
5073	950	pr.
5074 a	125	
b	225	
5075	175	
5076	250	
5077	1200	
5078	—	
5079	1200	
5080	325	
5081	—	
5082	325	
5083	100	
5084	100	
5085	1000	
5086	—	
5087	450	
5088	100	
5089	100	
5090	90	cover only
5091	750	
5092	750	
5093	25	
5094	55	
5095 a	250	
b	75	
5096	250	
5097	100	
5098	900	pr.
5099	45	
5100	850	
5101	25	
5102	70	
5103	225	
5104	750	
5105	450	
5106	525	
5107	500	
5108	—	

A GENERAL ASSORTMENT

Photo No.			
5109		60	
5110		85	
5111		100	
5112	a	185	
	b	500	
5113	a	575	
	b	600	
	c	575	
5114		7200	
5115	a	450	
	b	450	
	c	350	
	d	350	
5116		185	
5117		425	
5118		150	the set
5119		525	
5120		625	
5121		300	
5122		2750	
5123		4200	
5124		450	
5125		425	
5126		300	
5127		50	pr.
5128		50	pr.
5129		25	
5130		25	
5131		65	pr.
5132		50	pr.
5133		25	pr.
5134		40	ea. clear
		50	ea, white
		110	ea. blue
		110	ea. silver blue
5135		60	pr. knobs only
5136		55	pr.
5137		125	ea.
5138		25	pr. clear
		50	pr. fiery opalescent
		100	pr. canary
5139		—	
5140		50	ea.
5141		150	pr.
5142		30	ea.
5143		3	ea. with metal back
5144		3	ea. with metal back
5145		3	ea. with metal back
5146		3	ea. with metal back

Photo No.			
5147		—	
5148		—	
5149		75	ea.
5150		15	ea.
5151		100	
5152		100	
5153		300	ea. with fitting
5154		650	
5155		700	
5156		700	
5157		2250	
5158		2000	
5159		1000	
5160		1000	
5161		4200	the set
5162		450	
5163		4500	the set
5164		350	ea.
5165		40	
5166		85	ea. with brush
5167		750	
5168		400	
5169		65	clear
		225	blue
5170		125	
5171		20	ea.
5172		750	
5173		35	clear
		90	blue
5174		1000	blue
		1100	green
		900	black
5175		1000	blue
		1100	green
		900	black
5176	a	40	
5177		1200	clambroth (alabaster)
		1200	fiery opalescent
		1100	opaque white
		1400	blue
		1200	light amethyst
		2500	green
		3200	ruby
		1100	black
5178		5500	with stand
5179	a	550	
	b	450	
5180		500	
5181		40	

BOTTLES

The value of a bottle that retains its original paper label in excellent condition can be 250 percent of the value of a like bottle without its label.

Photo No.			
5182		250	
5183		180	clear
		300	clear with white stripes
		375	clear with blue trail
5184		180	clear
		300	clear with white stripes
		375	clear with blue trail
5185	a	1500	
	b	75	
5186		70	clear
		235	blue
		300	green
5187		35	clear
		160	fiery opalescent
		140	blue
		180	amethyst
		160	green
5188		35	clear
		160	fiery opalescent
		140	blue
		180	amethyst
		160	green
5189		35	clear
		160	fiery opalescent
		140	blue
		180	amethyst
		160	green
5190		35	clear
		160	fiery opalescent
		140	blue
		180	amethyst
		160	green
5191		350	with label
5192		45	clear
		210	opaque white
		250	blue
		250	amethyst
		275	green
5193		45	clear
		210	opaque white
		250	blue
		250	amethyst
		275	green
5194		750	
5195		250	ruby to clear
		275	blue to clear
		300	green to clear
5196		325	with label
5197	a	50	clear
		300	blue
		300	amethyst
		350	green
	b	60	clear
		280	blue
		300	pale amethyst
		380	green
	c	70	clear
		135	canary
		225	blue
5198	a	225	blue
		300	amethyst
		300	peacock green
	b	300	blue
		250	amethyst
		310	peacock green
	c	225	blue
		300	amethyst
		300	peacock green
5199		500	fiery opalescent
		400	blue
		450	amethyst
		650	green
		450	peacock green
5200		500	fiery opalescent
		400	blue
		450	amethyst
		650	green
		450	peacock green
5201		125	ea.
5202	a	100	with stopper
5203		125	with label
5204		85	
5205		25	bottle
5206		40	
5207	a	30	
	b	20	
5208	a	140	
	b	100	
	c	10	
5209		200	with rack
5210		180	
5211	a	65	
	b	75	
	c	85	
5212		110	without label
		400	with label